Blessing

Biblical Meaning and Pastoral Practice

Keith Grüneberg

Curate
Pangbourne with Tidmarsh and Sulham

GROVE BOOKS LIMITED
RIDLEY HALL RD CAMBRIDGE CB3 9HU

Contents

Acknowledgments

Some of the research on which this booklet is based was supported by the Arts and Humanities Research Board of the British Academy. Bible quotations are taken from the New Revised Standard Version.

The Cover Illustration is by Peter Ashton

First Impression March 2003
ISSN 1365-490X
ISBN 1 85174 526 2

Introduction

1

'Bless' and 'blessing' are words that Christians—or at least some Christians—use a lot.

I sometimes write 'God bless' at the end of a letter just before my signature. I had a friend who often said 'Bless you' when I had done something for him, as a way of expressing his thanks. 'It was such a blessing to me,' some people say when they have received something they found helpful. When someone sneezes 'Bless you' is a standard response. We talk about God blessing people, about people blessing each other and also about people blessing God. We have blessings at the end of many services—and in some churches only a priest is allowed to give a formal blessing. We may bless marriages, or wedding rings, or our food at meals, or the bread and wine at communion, or animals. But what is blessing? It is not a question we think about much. What should we bless? Who can bless?

As I found when researching for this booklet, quite a lot has been written on blessing in the Old Testament, a bit about blessing in the New Testament, but very little about how the biblical idea of blessing might apply to our life today. Blessing is not something that theologians seem to have paid much attention to.[1] But if we want to talk about blessing, or to do it, an idea of what we mean might be helpful.

This booklet attempts to explain what blessing means in the Bible, and to draw out some possible implications for modern Christian faith and practice. It is certainly not a full theological discussion of the theme. But my hope is that it will inform and stimulate further thought.

A word of caution. There are two words in the Old Testament often translated as 'bless.' This booklet is primarily concerned with the Hebrew root *brk* and its derivatives, and the Greek *eulogeo* and related words. The Hebrew word *'ashrê*, used to declare a person happy (for example, Psalm 1.1; Proverbs 28.14), will not be discussed; the Greek *makarios*, which has similar meaning, I mention only incidentally in chapter 3. This means that we will not be looking much at the Beatitudes ('Blessed are the poor in spirit...') from the Sermon on the Mount (Matthew 5.3–12), since they use the word *makarios*.

2 A Little Background– Especially to the Old Testament

This chapter can be skipped by anyone in a hurry to get to the 'answers.' However...

...it explains a little about the methodology which I will be applying; it gives some interesting evidence about blessing in Israel's neighbouring cultures; and it tries to show why the conclusions of this booklet are very different to those reached by many great scholars of the last century.

Etymology

People sometimes think that to find out the real meaning of a word you can look at its etymology, its derivation. For example someone might say that the word 'desperate' really means 'hopeless' since it is derived from the Latin word *spero* meaning 'hope' with the prefix *de* denoting the reversal of a process (as in 'decompose' or 'declassify'). In the case of 'desperate' this seems plausible, but other words show the limits of etymology. The word 'nice' ultimately derives from the Latin word *nescius* which means 'ignorant'—but when we call something or someone 'nice' nowadays we certainly do not mean that they do not know very much!

The reason for this is simply that the meaning of words can change over time. The English word 'bless' itself derives from the Old English *blēdsian* which probably meant 'mark with blood in order to consecrate.'[2] But for centuries now people who speak English have happily blessed without making any use of blood and used the word to translate *brk* in the Old Testament without thinking that this is all to do with blood.[3] To find out what a word means, we really need to look at how it is now used. It may have shaken off its history.

However, this principle can be pushed too far. Most words do not change their meanings as much as 'nice,' so derivation often is a good guide to meaning. Linguists dealing with a modern language can go and talk with people who speak the language, or may well have thousands of books to search through for more evidence of how the word is used. When investigating ancient Hebrew, limited to the Old Testament and a few other texts, we may need all the help we can get to establish what a word means. And linguists expect to explain how words change their meaning. If we cannot show how a word that we think once meant one thing could later come to mean something very different, it rather suggests that at least one of our proposed meanings is wrong.

What is Meaning?

Books have been written about the concept of meaning. Fortunately we do not need to worry about most of the issues. We just need to note three important points here:

1 A word can have several meanings. We do not have to fit every use of a word into one neat box. When we 'wait' for a bus we are doing something different from when we are employed by a restaurant to 'wait' on people having a meal. It is fairly easy to see how the same word could develop these two different senses, but we do not have to come up with one definition that fits both. The technical term for this is 'polysemy.' I shall be suggesting that 'blessing' is polysemous.

On the other hand, sometimes two or more unrelated words happen to be spelled the same (this is known as 'homonymy'). In English, a 'mole' can be a small mammal, a spot on the skin, a quantity in Chemistry, or a breakwater. In Hebrew the word meaning 'bless,' and the word meaning 'kneel' are both *brk*. Some scholars have tried to relate the two. For example, did people kneel to receive blessings? Is blessing connected to the idea of a child being accepted into a family by being taken onto an adult's knees, by its natural parents (Job 3.12) or by 'adoptive' parents (Gen 30.3; Gen 48.12; Gen 50.23)? But none of the suggested links has much evidence in its favour—and, for example, the idea that blessing is linked to the prosperity shown by a group of kneeling camels is frankly bizarre.[4] Homonymy seems a more likely explanation.

2 Meaning is not just a matter of denoting some thing or concept (as 'cat' denotes a certain kind of animal, or 'beauty' denotes the concept of attractiveness). 'Hello' does not denote anything, but obviously has meaning.

3 Meaning is not just a property of individual words. Often when words are put together into a sentence, or sentences into a larger unit, the whole takes on a meaning greater than the sum of the parts.

We can illustrate points (2) and (3) together. When we say 'Jesus is Lord' we may be saying that a concept of Lordship fits him. However, we are perhaps also committing ourselves to follow him, pledging allegiance to him. That may be just as much the meaning of our words. The importance of these last points will be particularly clear in chapter 4 below, when we consider whether saying 'bless you' was just a way of greeting or thanking.

Blessing in Israel's Neighbouring Cultures

In popular Arabic belief, the 'blessing' was regarded as an impersonal power that produces fertility and prosperity, and is mediated to the tribe by the father or tribal chief, or to men in their own neighbourhood by a holy person, without specifically mentioning God as its source or author.[5]

Based on this evidence, together with the assumption that religion always evolved from a primitive animistic religion, many scholars have argued that the roots of the Hebrew concept of blessing lie in some kind of power of fertility, which had no relation to God.[6] Many have also claimed that these roots are visible in parts of the Old Testament—for example, in the way that in Genesis 27 Isaac cannot retract his blessing. Once the blessing has been 'let loose,' so these scholars would say, no-one can control it. (For a different explanation, see chapter 4.)

However, evidence from Ugaritic, Phoenician-Punic and Aramaic tells a different story. This evidence is much older than the Arabic material we have just noted, and is much closer in time to the Old Testament. Texts written in these languages regularly make clear that blessing—for which they use a word etymologically related to the Hebrew word—is dependent on the activity of a god. Even when people bless they often explicitly call on a god to do something. The texts also make clear what blessing includes: 'the content of the blessing is long life, descendants, prosperity, success, and power.'[7] But they almost never use a noun 'blessing'—they talk about god(s) blessing and people blessing, but not about blessing as a concept or a force or a power in its own right. Etymology thus suggests that blessing in the Old Testament may well be about the divine gift of long life and prosperity, sometimes with people mediating this.

Etymology suggests that blessing in the OT may well be about the divine gift of long life and prosperity

What is Blessing? 3

The Old Testament

When God blesses in the Old Testament it often makes a material difference to people's lives. Genesis 24.35 implies that God's blessing on Abraham makes him wealthy. Proverbs 10.22 says that 'the blessing of the LORD makes rich.' The Old Testament does not confine God's activity to a spiritual realm distinct from the physical world, but sees God's hand at work in everything and expects God's favour to be apparent in every aspect of a person's life. (Of course the book of Job reminds us that things do not always work as neatly as that.) There is not normally any obvious and dramatic intervention, but things will go well.[8] Because for most people the most important things were having children and success in farming, blessing is often tied up with human, animal or plant fertility and growth—for example in Gen 1.22, 28; Lev 25.21; Deut 7.13. But it also brings wealth (as we have already seen), success over enemies (Gen 27.29; Deut 28.7),[9] and everything that makes for a good life (Ps 133.1–3). In the Old Testament blessing brings all-round prosperity or well-being.

In the Old Testament blessing brings all-round prosperity or well-being

In fact, the great majority of the results of blessing that the Old Testament refers to are material. But there are some exceptions. Deuteronomy 28.1–14, for example, lists all the blessings that God promises the people of Israel as long as they are obedient. Most of them are to do with success in agriculture and in gaining wealth—and in having children—but v 9 includes the promise that Israel will be God's holy people. In Numbers 6.24–6 the primary blessing offered is simply God's grace and favour, though this was meant to result in protection (v 24) and prosperity (the word translated 'peace' in v 26 is the Hebrew word *shalom*, which means all-round well-being).

Blessing is at least predominantly something for humans. When blessing is said to be upon things, plants or animals this is normally a way of saying that their owners will benefit from them. When God tells the Israelites in Exodus 23.25 that if they are obedient 'I will bless your bread and your water,' he clearly means that he will give them a plentiful supply of food and water. The same applies in Deuteronomy 28.5 'Blessed shall be your basket and your kneading bowl.' This means that there will be plenty of crops for the people to gather and make into bread; it does not make the basket and bowl in any way special in themselves. In Psalm 65.10 God blesses the growth of the field—but the verse before tells us that at least part of the purpose of this is to provide grain for humans. Deuteronomy 28.4 mentions domestic animals bearing young, but the point is that their owners will benefit from this, as from the crops in their fields and from having children themselves. So, to restate what I said at the beginning of this paragraph: *blessing in the Old Testament is predominantly about human well-being, even when expressed as blessing on things, plants or animals.*

However, the beginning of Genesis may give us pause for thought. Here God blesses the birds and sea creatures (1.22) and the seventh day (2.3) as well as humans (1.28). The blessing on the seventh day is probably saying that the day of rest will benefit everything that has been created. The tricky question is how much the rest of creation exists for the sake of humanity, and how much it has value in its own right, or for its relationship to God independent of humanity. Humanity is the crown of creation; the ongoing story of Genesis focuses on humans; 1.14 tells us that the heavenly bodies are created in part for their use to humans in marking times and seasons. On the other hand, it is not obvious that every creature blessed benefits humans—what about the great sea monsters mentioned in v 21? While we may think of their importance to the overall ecosystem, that would not have been an issue when Genesis was written. So, does the beginning of Genesis suggest that animals can be blessed for their own sake, or is the point only that they will be fertile as if they belonged to a blessed person?

Blessing in the OT is predominantly about human well-being

The New Testament

The New Testament, as we might expect, links God's blessing to Jesus. God 'has blessed us in Christ with every spiritual blessing' (Eph 1.3). It is in Christ Jesus that the blessing promised to Abraham comes to the Gentiles (Gal 3.14). God sent Jesus to bless his people in turning them from their wicked ways (Acts 3.25). Because of Jesus, and especially his death and resurrection, God can give to humans what is most important for their well-being.

Does this mean that blessing has become 'spiritualized'? I do not think there is ever any intention to contrast the blessings of the new covenant with the more concrete blessings generally found in the Old Testament.[10] Ephesians 1.3, for example, says that Christians receive in Christ every spiritual blessing in the heavenly places, but does not say that present material blessings are no longer possible.[11] Hebrews 6.7 talks about God's blessing being upon the ground which produces a useful crop. What is certainly the case, however, is that in the New Testament as a whole the value of the things of this life has been relativized. The life we will have when God's kingdom has fully come is far more significant than what happens to us now; as Paul says, 'I consider that the sufferings of this present time are not worth comparing with the glory about to be revealed to us' (Rom 8.18). The New Testament ideal is still a happy and prosperous life without suffering—a bodily life (1 Cor 15), shared with the rest of creation (Rom 8.19ff), on a renewed earth (Rev 21.1). But it is more concerned that people should enjoy this forever in the future, than that they should have it for a few years now. So in the Beatitudes (Matt 5.3–12) the people who are blessed[12] may have a difficult time now, mourning, suffering persecution and so on, but they can confidently look forward to being comforted, seeing God and inheriting the earth.

Because of Jesus, God can give to humans what is most important for their well-being

Many of the good things that Christians can enjoy now are foretastes of this future life, since God's kingdom is already breaking in to the present. We live in the overlap between the coming of the kingdom in Jesus and the end of the present age. (According to the New Testament, eternal life begins now. The change to which we look forward is not the start of the new age, but the end of the old.) The presence of the Holy Spirit, which Gal 3.14 links closely with blessing, is itself a sign and guarantee (2 Cor 1.22; 5.5; Eph 1.14) of the kingdom.[13] And the Holy Spirit gives us many things to make our lives now better, both 'spiritual' such as joy and peace, and sometimes material (such as healing). The Spirit carries on the ministry of Jesus, who certainly did not ignore people's bodily needs even though his main focus was on calling them to repent and believe in the good news of the kingdom.

Present material goods come lower down the scale of values in the New Testament than they do in much of the Old Testament. That does not mean that they are completely unimportant—the New Testament calls us to social action as well as to evangelism—but it does mean that other things are more important.

Some Big Questions

Where does all this leave us? In my mind it raises some significant questions. The first question is simply: can we actually see signs of God's blessing in the world around us? Does it look as though people receive God's blessing and do well as a result? We are not necessarily looking for miraculous happenings, but do we think that a farmer may have a particularly good yield from his fields because God has blessed him? If we bless someone (see next chapter) is it simply a pious wish or might it make a difference? This same question is raised by any intercessory prayer; if we think that, for example, praying for someone who is ill to get better may make a difference to that person's recovery, we are saying that God may speed or enhance the healing processes as a result of our prayer. Most Christians have examples of praying for someone who did recover unexpectedly well from their ailment. And sometimes studies are published which aim to provide statistical evidence that people who are prayed for do recover better than those who are not. But it is well-nigh impossible to demonstrate conclusively that prayer makes much difference in this way; if it could be proved, I am sure that prayer and Christian faith in general would be a lot more popular!

Can we actually see signs of God's blessing in the world around us?

One reason why it is tempting to stress non-material blessings and future blessings is that we then do not have to worry about some of the problems that arise with present material blessings. We do not have to ask why faithful African Christians may be facing starvation, though they surely 'ought' to be receiving God's blessing, while many atheists in the western world live in comfort (alongside, of course, many western Christians); we simply deny the relevance of present material prosperity to blessing. However, there are two difficulties with this. The first is that I do not think it does justice to the biblical material we have looked at. And the second is that unless we think that God just does not care about people's pain now or does not ever do anything about it, we do not get rid of the problem by saying that blessing is spiritual and future. The problem is still there; we have just taken the easy way out by trying to avoid it in this case.

If we are to respect both what we read in the Bible and what we see in the world, we need to accept that things are complicated. God does care about people's present physical well-being, and does act sometimes to enhance this. He regularly works through the normal processes of nature, which after all he designed and which he still keeps in being. Often too he acts through human beings. Sometimes he may act miraculously; sometimes he may simply make the natural forces work better than they normally do. But often—to our human minds it frequently seems too often—he appears to do little or nothing. And theologians have spent much time working out why that is, since it is part of the classic problem of evil. But we can at least say that since present material prosperity is only a part of blessing, those who lack it may well still be blessed. They may

If we bless someone is it simply a pious wish or might it make a difference?

indeed have the things that are most important for their well-being whatever else they may lack, for they may know that an eternal life without suffering awaits them.

And we also need to think about the place of animals. We have seen that the Old Testament may suggest that they have value in their own right, though this is not terribly clear. But even if this is not what Genesis 1 is concerned with, we might still argue that all of creation is intrinsically worthwhile (which is why God wants to liberate it, as Rom 8.21 suggests) and that an animal's prosperity would matter to God (perhaps implied by the vision of peace between animals in Isa 11.6–8). If so, perhaps we should still think about God blessing animals for their own sake, even though the Bible does not explicitly talk about it.

4 Blessing People

The Old Testament

In this chapter we consider what happens when one human blesses another. We begin with three passages in the Old Testament.

1. In Numbers 6.22–27 instructions are given to Israel's priests about how they are to bless the people. They are to call on YHWH (the name of Israel's God, usually written as 'LORD' in most Bibles) to show favour to the people and prosper them. When the priests do this—described in v 23 as their blessing the people—YHWH himself will bless the people. The priests can expect their blessings to make a difference because YHWH promises that he will bless when they utter these words. This does not make the words magic, or give the priests any magic power. It is all about God's promise. (A comparison with Holy Communion might be helpful here. We benefit from participation in it not because it is magic, but because God promises that he will give grace to those who do certain things with faith.)

2. Genesis 26.34–28.9 tells the story of Jacob tricking his father Isaac into blessing him, when Isaac wanted to bless Esau instead. The story stresses the human power to bless. Once Isaac has blessed Jacob he cannot withdraw that blessing but as he tells Esau 'I have blessed him—and blessed he shall be' (v 33). All he can give Esau is a half-blessing (vv 39–40), offering some comfort but not the riches given to Jacob (vv 27–29). The rest of Genesis shows Jacob getting the prosperity with which he had been blessed. Human blessings thus make a difference. Equally it is clear that Isaac invokes God's activity in blessing his son (vv 27–29). We must also remember that the wider story, especially 25.21–23, makes clear that God wanted Jacob to be pre-eminent over Esau.

But why cannot Isaac withdraw the blessing? The most likely explanation is that when one has just performed a formal act, it is no good to say 'Sorry—I did not mean it. Let us forget it and start again.' When Isaac has just given a father's blessing to his son he cannot simply change his mind. Similarly in Genesis 29, when Jacob marries Leah thinking that he is getting Rachel, no-one seems to think that his mistaken belief invalidates the wedding; he just is married to Leah, and nothing can alter that. We may or may not think this principle, that a mistaken belief makes no difference to what has happened, is defensible. Perhaps we would be more sympathetic if our present culture put less emphasis on the individual doing whatever he or she wants, and more on keeping one's word and building up the structures of society. Even in our law courts once the jury has come to a decision and given its verdict none of the jurors can do anything to change that verdict; on the other hand, divorce is readily available and generally accepted without the need to provide much justification. But the main point for our discussion of Genesis 27 is that we can explain what happens without making blessing a force independent of God.

3. Numbers 22–24, the story of Balaam, again shows the power in human blessings. Balak, the Moabite king, summons Balaam to curse Israel, since Balak believes that if Balaam does this Israel will become vulnerable in battle. Yнwн's obvious concern to make sure that Balaam does not curse suggests that Balak is not fundamentally misguided in his beliefs about the potential power of cursing. So Balak is very annoyed when Balaam does what God wants, and blesses the Israelites instead of cursing them—making it even less likely that Moab could defeat them in battle.

But what makes Balaam's words a blessing? They look more like a prophecy, saying what God is going to do, rather than an invocation of God's favour. Balaam does not say 'May God make Israel numerous,' but says 'Who can count the dust of Jacob, or number the dust-cloud[14] of Israel?' (23.10). Probably this is because Balaam has the authority of a prophet to speak for God. So when he says something God is committed to doing it. Similarly in Genesis 49, when Jacob on his deathbed blesses his sons, he does this by making statements about their future.[15]

What Do These Passages Show?

1 Humans can have a real power to bless. The priests, Isaac and Balaam do not just ask God to bless the people, but actually invoke blessing—when they utter words of blessing, those blessed do receive benefits.

2 Blessing is not separate from God. God is involved in giving the benefits. God controls those who give blessings.

3 The power to bless is not intrinsic to humans, but is granted to them by God. God commits himself to giving blessing in response to human words.

But which human words? Or rather, whose words? Can everyone authoritatively invoke God's blessing on others? Or is it only priests in the temple, fathers on their deathbeds, prophets, and perhaps a few other people in special circumstances, who can do this?

It is normally impossible to be sure whether an 'everyday' blessing in the Old Testament was meant to be an effective invocation of God's blessing, or whether it is instead simply a request to God to give his blessing, in other words a prayer. When in Ruth 2.4 Boaz greets his reapers with 'The LORD be with you' and they reply 'The LORD bless you' do they think they are asking God to bless, or declaring God's blessing? When Rebekah's brothers bless her, saying 'May you become thousands of myriads; may your offspring gain possession of the gates of their enemies' (Gen 24.60) are they just asking God to do this for her, or are their words more than a request?

> *God gives humans a real power to bless— but not in such a way that he has to reward the wicked*

Two things suggest to me that at least some 'everyday' blessings were not just prayers. First, there is the fact that they are often addressed not to God but to the person being blessed. Genesis 24.60, which we have just mentioned, illustrates this: 'May you become thousands of myriads' is not an obvious way to ask God to do this for her, particularly as the Hebrew can more literally be translated simply 'Become thousands of myriads' (see also 1 Samuel 23.21). Secondly, I do not think it asks too much of the spiritual discernment of ordinary people to expect them to recognize that, for example, those who have just done them some good turn (Deut 24.13), or a fellow-pilgrim (Ps 118.26) merit God's blessing, and so they can declare it. Of course there may be other reasons why God does not want to prosper the person blessed—the man who restores the cloak to the poor man in Deut 24.13 *may* be an adulterer who worships other gods as well as YHWH. But when the priests bless in the temple, they do not enquire into the lives of everyone present; it appears to be presumed that the blessing will not be received if someone goes away and ignores God in how they subsequently live. God gives humans a real power to bless—but not in such a way that he has to reward the wicked.

Blessings were often given when people met each other (Ruth 2.4; 1 Samuel 15.13) or went away (Genesis 24.60 again; Genesis 28.1–5; 31.55; 47.10; 2 Samuel 19.39). The first and last thing people said to each other was 'May God prosper you.' So 'bless' is the standard Hebrew word for greeting, or saying farewell—and is often translated thus in modern versions in for example 1 Samuel 13.10 and 2 Kings 4.29. Some people wonder whether the word became used so often in these contexts that people forgot what it originally meant—in the same way that most people say 'Bless you' following a sneeze without thinking that the words could be an invocation of God's blessing. The English word 'Goodbye' derives from the custom of saying 'God be with you' when people parted from one another; this phrase was said so often, and people came to think so little about it, that it was shortened to a word which makes no obvious reference to God. However, it seems very unlikely that *all* nuance of blessing was *always* ignored when the Hebrew word was used in these contexts. People did, at least sometimes, genuinely bless each other when they met or parted.

Similar arguments apply when people offered a blessing as a way of thanking someone who had helped them (for example, Deut 24.13; Ruth 3.10; 1 Sam 23.21) or as a way of praising someone (for example, Gen 14.19; 1 Kings 1.47). The best thing that you can wish for a person who has done you a good turn, or for someone who has done something worthy of praise, is that they receive God's blessing. Probably the word 'bless' came to mean no more than 'thank' or 'praise' in the minds of some people. But surely others would have wanted to invoke God's blessing as they acknowledged what the person they are thanking or praising had done. Certainly in 1 Kings 1.47 the way David's servants bless/praise/congratulate him is by asking God's favour for his son Solomon.

The New Testament

Some scholars try to claim that the New Testament marks a significant shift from the Old.[16] Three things can be said against this:

1 The New Testament certainly has much less to say than the Old about human blessings. But the practice seems to continue. Jesus tells his disciples to bless those who curse them (Luke 6.28), and this command is echoed by Paul (Rom 12.14; 1 Cor 4.12) and in 1 Peter 3.9. Jesus himself blesses little children (Mark 10.16), and blesses his disciples when he finally parts from them at his ascension (Luke 24.50–51). The 'closing prayers' at the end of some of the letters should perhaps also be classed as blessings—Hebrews 13.20–21 is often used as a blessing in churches today; so too is the 'Grace' (2 Cor 13.13). Letters also often start with a greeting that could be a blessing (for example, Rom 1.7 'Grace to you and peace from God our Father and the Lord Jesus Christ').

2 Christ's coming makes a difference to how God blesses the world (see chapter 3 above). But there seems no good reason why this should abolish the practice of human blessing. The blessings humans invoke in the Old Testament often echo God's blessings given

in Genesis 1—God apparently fulfils his purpose through human invocations of blessing. (Barth claims that blessings in the Old Testament pick up only God's blessing of Abraham. But this seems arbitrary; and in any case Gen 9.25–7 makes clear that human cursing and blessing could occur before Abraham's time.[17]) Why should God not seek human cooperation in extending the blessing now available in Christ—just as he asks for our prayers in extending his kingdom?

3 There is a danger of undervaluing the Old Testament. Even if the New Testament made no mention of human blessings, we should assume that what the Old Testament said remains valid—unless we had strong reasons to think that something in the New Testament pointed in a different direction. The Old Testament is not just background to the New—telling us how to interpret its references to human blessing—but Scripture in its own right.

Before we move on, a brief note is called for on Hebrews 7.7, 'It is beyond dispute that the inferior is blessed by the superior.' This is meant as a statement of the obvious, derived from the Old Testament (and so not a new Christian rule). But in the Old Testament bless-ers are often not superior to those they bless; we may think of the poor man blessing the person who returned his cloak (Deut 24.13), or David's servants blessing him (1 Kings 1.47). So probably Hebrews refers only to the most formal settings, when people have well-defined roles—in worship the priest blesses the worshippers, not *vice versa*, and at a deathbed the father blesses his children. Authority to invoke God's blessing here goes with authority in role. The fact that Melchizedek blessed Abraham—and that Abraham gave him a tithe—shows that even the patriarch recognized Melchizedek's authority as priest.

Blessing People Today

Probably the first thing that comes to mind when we think of one person blessing another today is the blessing often given at the end of a service. The purpose of having it there is to make the point that God's favour goes with the worshippers as they go out into their daily life and work. In Jewish tradition the priestly blessing was given to worshippers as they departed from the Temple; although this is not explicitly commanded in Numbers 6, it is certainly consistent with it.

It seems entirely right that it should be the person who has presided over the worship—thus taking on a particular role and authority within the congregation, at least for that service—who should invoke God's blessing. In

Anglicanism, as in the Roman Catholic church, it is only priests who are given authority to bless; deacons and lay ministers who take services may ask God to bless all present, including themselves ('may the Lord bless us…'), but not invoke God's blessing on others ('the Lord bless you…'). How many people in the congregation notice the difference in the wording is of course another question! Whether or not it is right that only priests, and not others authorized to lead worship, should invoke blessing depends rather more on the view taken about priesthood and leadership in the church than on anything about blessing, so cannot be discussed here.

Blessing in the Bible was part of everyday life. We have seen that it was not just priests or those with particular authority who invoked or asked for God's blessing on others. Anyone could do it. It was especially common when people met or parted. It was also used as a way *These are things that we could well rediscover today* of thanking or praising someone. It seems to me that these are things we could well continue or rediscover today—making clear to ourselves and to others that what we most want is for them to enjoy God's blessing. 'God bless' at the end of a letter can be a pious platitude, or just a conventional phrase like 'Yours faithfully.' But why not conclude what you have to say with a reminder of what is actually most important? Why not bless the person who has just helped you with something? Why not bless a child when putting him or her to bed at night? When I discussed with my bishop the fact that I was writing this booklet, he told me about something he had seen while on holiday on Italy. A Roman Catholic priest had been visiting his parents and now the time had come for him to return to his parish. It was therefore time for a blessing to be given. So the priest knelt down, and his father blessed him. The priest had the authority to bless in worship, but within the family it was the father's role to bless his son as he departed. I hope that on other occasions the son blessed his parents too.

And we do not just ask God to bless. We invoke or declare his blessing. We believe that God always wants to bless humans—at least provided they remain faithful to him.[18] We may need to be more tentative about the form that blessing will take. We can always invoke the blessing of God's peace on a person, for example; equally we can always invoke blessing on someone in *We do not just ask— we invoke or declare God's blessing* his or her marriage. It requires more discernment to know when to invoke success in a business venture, or when to invoke the blessing of children on a childless couple. Sometimes it is doubtless right to remain at the level of generalities. When blessing a group this is almost inevitable. But Old

Testament blessings certainly did not always remain at that level (for example, Genesis 27.27–9; Num 22–4); and in our prayer we often try to be specific.

But does it actually make any difference? Do people have a better life because at the end of a service a blessing was invoked on them than they would have had otherwise? If we started to bless those we met, would things change for them?[19] I think it is unlikely that we would notice dramatic results most of the time—just as our prayers often do not have dramatic results. There is no sign that people in the Bible expected striking results from their blessings. But they blessed in the faith that God does want to use humans to mediate his grace.

Blessing God

What do we mean when we talk of blessing God?

In the Bible people are often said to bless God or his name (Genesis 24.48; 1 Chronicles 29.10, 20; Psalm 16.7; 103.1–2, 20–22; James 3.9 etc), or God is called blessed (Genesis 24.27; 1 Kings 5.7; Ezra 7.27; Psalm 28.6; Rom 1.5; 1 Peter 1.3 etc). This means simply that God is thanked or praised—in every case we could replace the word 'bless' with 'thank' or 'praise' and what we end up with would make perfect sense. Sometimes what 'bless' means is particularly clear, on the principle that a word's meaning can be shown by the company it keeps.[20] In Psalm 145.2 the Psalmist says he will *bless God* every day, and *praise his name* for ever. In v 10 all God's works will *give him thanks*, and all his faithful will *bless him*. In Psalm 96.2, *blessing God's name* is connected to *singing to him* and *declaring his salvation*. The angels in Revelation 7.12 ascribe to God 'blessing and glory and wisdom and thanksgiving and honour and power and might'; there are similar lists in 5.12 and 13.[21]

Talk of blessing God in the modern church generally follows the biblical usage

We have already seen, in chapter 4, that people sometimes thanked or praised each other using the word 'bless.' The use of the word for praising or thanking God probably arose by analogy from this. It hardly seems likely that ancient Israelites, or the Jews and Christians who followed them, believed they could make God more prosperous by their words, or bestow any other benefit on him. Of course it is good theology that God desires our praise and thanks. It is also good theology that praise and thanks is an appropriate response when God has blessed us. But the biblical usage of the word 'bless' in itself does not draw attention to either of these points.

Talk of blessing God in the modern church generally follows the biblical usage. It often occurs in what we sing—for example, the hymns 'Stand up and bless the Lord' or 'All people that on earth do dwell' (verse 3 contains the line 'Praise, laud and bless his name always'), the Taizé chant 'Bless the Lord, my soul,' the songs beginning 'Blessèd be the name of the Lord.'[22] Many of these draw more or less directly from the Bible, so it is not surprising that they follow its idioms. Anglicans may know the call and response 'Let us bless the Lord'—'Thanks be to God' sometimes said at the end of a service. In this the minister calls on the people to praise and thank God, and they respond by doing so. In my experience God is also often blessed in prayer, liturgical and free, prepared and spontaneous, in services and outside.

However, a slightly different usage appears in Matt Redman's popular song 'When the music fades.'[23] This begins:

> When the music fades,
> all is stripped away,
> and I simply come;
> longing just to bring
> something that's of worth,
> that will bless your heart.

Here it is suggested that our heartfelt praise will please God. As we have noted above, this is good theology, but not part of what the Bible means by blessing God (and the Bible nowhere talks about blessing God's heart). There is nothing intrinsically wrong about extending the use of the word—to be different from the Bible in linguistic usage is not to be unbiblical. On the other hand, I am not sure that anything is gained by this extension; 'bless your heart' does not say anything that 'warm your heart' would not, unless the latter is too anthropomorphic. And the danger of extending the meaning of a word is that we may mistakenly find the new meaning where it does not belong; we may think, for example, that the Psalmist is thinking about pleasing God when he is just concerned with praising him.

Blessing Things

6

Blessings at Meals

The standard Jewish form of a grace, in other words a prayer of thanksgiving for food, was—and is—something like 'Blessed are you, Lord God, King of the Universe, who has caused bread to come forth from the earth,' 'Blessed are you, Lord our God, who has created the fruit of the vine,' and so on.[24] In other words, they bless God for the food, and as we have seen in the last chapter this means simply thanking him for it. The earliest evidence for such graces is probably found in 1 Samuel 9.13, which talks about Samuel needing to bless a sacrifice before the people can eat. There is no reason why the sacrifice itself should need a prophet to bless it,[25] but the people want their great religious leader to say grace before they tuck in to the meat from the sacrifice and the rest of their meal. 'Blessing the food' is a shorthand way of saying 'blessing God for the food.'

So when the New Testament refers to blessings at meals it is probably this way of thanking God that is referred to. Blessings are mentioned in the accounts of the feeding of the five thousand and the four thousand (Matt 14.19; Mark 6.41; 8.7; Luke 9.16), the Last Supper (Matt 26.26; Mark 14.22), Jesus' meal at Emmaus (Luke 24.30) and the Corinthian church's sharing in communion (1 Cor 10.16). The same authors also use the Greek word *eucharisteo*, which means 'give thanks' (and from which our word 'Eucharist' is derived) to describe what Jesus did at these meals (Matt 15.36; 26.27; Mark 8.6; 14.23; Luke 22.17, 19; 1 Cor 11.24). We know that at Jewish Passover meals there was a 'cup of blessing,' following the Jewish custom of blessing God, and 1 Cor 10.16 is clearly following this usage. If we think this says that Jesus 'blesses' the bread in the same way that he blesses people, or 'consecrates' it, we are misinterpreting what the New Testament actually says.

When God is thanked for food, does it not make the food special?

But when God is thanked for food, does it not make the food special? In acknowledging that the food before us is part of what God gives us, and then if we ask him to nourish us through it, do not we make our lives even richer, even more full of blessing? We may not be adding some extra magical power to the food, changing it into something else, but things are not quite the same after the prayer as they were before it. In blessing God for what we are about to eat, do not we at least ask God to bless us through it? The answer is obviously—yes, of course we do, and particularly in a communion service.[26] So does it much matter whether we think we are thanking God or blessing something? I think it does, for two reasons. Firstly it makes sure we do not think we are *primarily* doing something to the food, or the bread and wine at communion. But secondly there is something I recently learned from Jewish tradition. In the Tosefta (which dates from around AD 250) it says that 'One who makes enjoyable use of the world without saying a blessing over it is guilty of profane use of sanctified matter.'[27] Everything in the natural world

By acknowledging that it is God's we gain the right to use it for our good

already belongs to God; we do not need to make it more holy before we can eat it, but instead by acknowledging that it is God's we gain the right to use it for our good. We do not say grace because there is something wrong with material things but because there is something right about them.

Blessing Crops, Animals and Businesses

We saw in chapter 3 that in the Old Testament God is said to bless things, and especially plants and animals, and that at least normally this is a shorthand way of saying that he blesses people by giving them food and wealth. We might well then expect that people would ask for God's blessing to be upon things, again as a shorthand way of asking that they be a source of prosperity to their owner. This would be no different to simply praying for a good harvest, except if blessing is effectively invoked on the thing, not just prayed for. However, there are only a couple of clear examples of this happening, in Deuteronomy 26.15, 33.9 and 33.11. In the first and last of these it is land that is blessed; in the middle one it is the tribe of Levi's 'substance,' its wealth and other resources which enable it to live. It would certainly seem permissible, then, for Christians to bless land that it might be fruitful, or even a business that it might provide a livelihood to its owner and employees. It is permissible as long as we remember that it is really the people who are being blessed—and for this reason it may sometimes be better to try to phrase what we are doing as a blessing on people ('bless Joanne and all who work in this business'; 'bless the farmers of our area with a good harvest…').

When it comes to blessing animals, our practice will depend on how we answer the questions posed at the end of chapter 3. We can certainly bless farm animals in the same way that we can bless crops. If we bless pets it will have to be because we consider that they have a value in their own right, and so God wants their prosperity for its own sake; or because we think they increase their owner's well-being enough that blessing the animal is an indirect way to bless the owner. Since I know the difference that the affection and companionship of a pet can give, particularly to an elderly person, I would encourage even anyone who does not see independent value in animals not to reject completely the idea of pet blessings.

Blessing Other Things

a) Houses

The normal Hebrew word for 'house,' *bayit*, sometimes denotes the building, but often means either the household—the people connected with a house—or the domestic economy. So Old Testament references to blessing houses often mean no more than 'bless this family' (2 Sam 6.11–12; Psalm 115.12) or 'bless this person with prosperity' (Gen 39.5). The word *naweh* used in Proverbs 3.33 where God 'blesses the abode of the righteous' does at least normally refer to the place where a person—or animal—lives. But it still seems likely that the blessing is really on the righteous person in his or her home, not on the building in itself.

So it would seem entirely right, for example, when someone moves into a new house to ask that they be blessed while they live there. And if this comes out as 'bless this house, that it may be a place of peace and love…' the Old Testament would seem to suggest that this is all right. House-blessings carried out in response to poltergeist or other paranormal activity raise too many issues to discuss properly here;[28] all that can be said is that if they are to be blessings in the biblical sense their ultimate focus must be on the people of the house, not the place itself. Perhaps it would be helpful if we thought of *home*-blessings, not *house*-blessings.

b) Marriages

There is no direct biblical evidence for blessings at weddings. But it is hard to imagine that a couple were not blessed at their marriage. Everyone's hope would be that the marriage would add to the couple's well-being (not least through their having children) and so God's blessing would be invoked. To bless a marriage is to ask that the couple be blessed by it, which we would surely want to do. In passing we should note that, since we can scarcely ask God to prosper something of which we think he disapproves, if a church offers a blessing on a particular marriage it implies that it does not consider this marriage contrary to God's will. In my opinion little or no purpose is served if a church refuses to marry a couple (perhaps because one of them has been divorced) but instead offers to bless them.

c) Wedding Rings

If we speak of blessing a wedding ring, we are moving some way beyond the biblical usage of the word 'bless.' What we are doing is asking that the ring be a symbol of the couple's love and of their vows, which will strengthen their marriage, and thus benefit them. The ring is thus to be a way in which God blesses them, but only with several intermediate stages. It is not obvious that anything is gained by talking about blessing here—and it can only encourage people to think that blessing can somehow make objects special—when we could just speak of dedicating the rings. But equally it is not exactly wrong to do so. It would not be wrong either simply to accept that the word 'bless' in English can mean 'dedicate' or 'consecrate'; as we noted above (page 20) it is not being unbiblical to differ from the Bible in linguistic usage. But, again as there, I just think that using the word in this way is more likely to be confusing than helpful.

d) Blessing and Consecration

In other cases too it may be better to speak of dedication or consecration than of blessing. If oils for use in anointing, or the water to be used in a baptism, are 'blessed' it is at least clear that they are being set apart for use in ways that will mediate God's blessing to people. But there has not been some power of blessing transferred into them. If new kneelers in a church are 'blessed' then I guess they will help those who use them to pray, and this will lead to blessing. But here—and I think the same would apply to most other things for church use—the blessing is so indirect that as with wedding rings it hardly seems the most important thing to think about when what we really want to do is thank God for them and dedicate them for their new use.

Conclusion 7

In our brief survey we have not been able to look at everything to do with blessing.

We have not considered at all what sort of words should be used in a blessing—or whether it is possible to bless without using words. We have not thought about the use of gesture, such as making the sign of the cross or laying hands on the person to be blessed. What we have done is look at the heart of blessing, and found that it is to do with God making humans prosper or do well. This has both material and non-material implications, since human well-being has both physical and non-physical aspects. And God gives to humans the authority to invoke his blessing, in both formal and informal situations. Blessing proper is for humans (and perhaps animals), but we can speak of blessing things when this is a shorthand way of talking about those things contributing to human well-being. However, sometimes this is likely to be confusing rather than helpful. We can also talk of blessing God, since this means thanking or praising him. We might think that this could cause confusion too, but the usage is so well established both in the Bible and in the church that it can hardly be changed.

My hope is that this booklet will help to clear up some of the confusion around blessing, so that we understand better what God does for us and for the world, and so that we can be better agents of his blessing. May God bless all who read it!

Notes

1 For example, neither the *New Dictionary of Theology* nor *A New Dictionary of Christian Theology* have even a short article about blessing. 'Blessing' does not appear in the index of the systematic theologies of Berkhof, Grudem, McGrath, Pannenberg or Wainwright, amongst many others.

If you want to do some more reading about blessing, the following would be good starting points:

A Thiselton, 'The Supposed Power of Words in the Biblical Writings' *Journal of Theological Studies* 25 (1974) pp 283–299

C Westermann, *Blessing in the Bible and the Life of the Church* (Philadelphia: Fortress Press, 1978)—this will give a different view on many issues to that of this booklet.

The works mentioned in the notes will also give you plenty to think about, as will commentaries on the relevant passages! But the topic has not received as much attention as it should.

2 T Hoad (ed), *The Concise Oxford Dictionary of English Etymology* (Oxford: OUP, 1996).

3 It is true that, theologically, Christians may wish to link blessing with Christ's blood. However, this is not part of the word's basic meaning; Jews and Christians might agree on what the word 'blessing' means (as this booklet will be arguing, one central meaning is something like 'God's favour resulting in human prosperity'), but would obviously disagree on whether it has anything to do with Christ.

4 References to those who have seriously advanced this view are found in C Mitchell, *The Meaning of brk 'to bless' in the Old Testament* (Atlanta: Scholars Press, 1987) pp 13, 15.

5 J Scharbert, '*brk; brkh*' in *Theological Dictionary of the Old Testament II* (Grand Rapids: Eerdmans, 1975) pp 283-4.

6 Important studies on blessing which take this view have been contributed by such scholars as Pedersen, Mowinckel, Hempel, Wehmeier and Westermann.

7 Scharbert, *op cit*, p 283.

8 'God usually blesses by making the natural processes work better than they normally do, rather than by circumventing them' (Mitchell, *op cit*, p 39).

9   It is not much good to become well off, then lose everything to an enemy.

10 Dividing things into separate 'material' and 'spiritual' categories, such that
    material things are by definition not spiritual and *vice versa*, has happened in
    the last few centuries as a result of the Enlightenment, and is not the
    worldview of the New Testament authors. 1 Cor 15.44 with its talk of spiritual
    bodies suggests that at least here 'spiritual' means more 'to do with the human
    in relationship with God' than 'immaterial' (see also 1 Cor 2.14-15). Similarly,
    in Rom 7.14 the law which is 'spiritual' is contrasted with Paul's fleshly, that is
    sinful, state.

11 The fact that the blessing here is 'in the heavenly places' shows that it is not to
    do with present material goods. 'Spiritual' may mean simply 'given by the
    Holy Spirit' (*eg* A Lincoln, *Ephesians* [Dallas: Word Books, 1990] p 19), or
    'relating to the human spirit,' or 'linked to the divine/human relationship' (see
    previous note).

12 As we noted in chapter 1, the word here is *makarios*.

13 If I were writing a full theology of blessing, I would want to say more about
    how Father, Son and Holy Spirit are all involved; like so much in Christian
    theology, it can only be fully understood in Trinitarian terms. That is why
    formal blessings normally explicitly refer to the blessing of God, Father, Son
    and Spirit.

14 Other translations have 'fourth part.'

15 By no means everything he says is good; the blessing that can be given depends
    on what is right for the person receiving it, not just on what the bless-er may
    want.

16 For example Karl Barth and Wolfgang Schenk.

17 In Hebrew, v 26a says 'Blessed be the Lᴏʀᴅ, the God of Shem'; so it is not
    explicitly said that Noah 'blesses' any of his sons. However, v 26b and v 27 are
    clear blessings, even if not explicitly labelled thus.

18 And, as I suggested above (p 14), it is not the bless-er's responsibility to
    establish this before uttering the blessing.

19 See Timothy Pain, *Blessing and Curse* (Eastbourne: Kingsway, 1987).

20 The reason for this is that the more closely related things are, the more likely
    they are to be spoken about together. Modern linguistics discusses this under
    the heading 'collocation.'

21 There is not the space here to consider whether there is some particular nuance
    in the word 'bless' or whether it is just a general word for praising or thanks-
    giving. I cautiously favour the latter; but see S Dawes, '"Bless the Lord": An
    invitation to affirm the living God' *Expository Times*, 106.10 (1995) pp 293-6.

22 *Complete Mission Praise* 808 and 809, and elsewhere.

23 *Complete Mission Praise* 1016 and elsewhere.

24 See, for example, the Mishnaic tractate *Berakoth, ie* 'blessings,' sections 6-8.

25 And if it did the people would have to wait a considerable time after he had blessed it before they could eat, since the meat would have to be cooked.

26 C Buchanan, *Eucharistic Consecration* (Grove Worship booklet W 148) argues that whatever your doctrine of communion it is almost inevitable to talk about some kind of consecration taking place.

27 *T Berakoth* 4.1; I owe the reference and the point I make to L A Hoffman, 'Blessings and Their Translations in Current Jewish Liturgies' *Worship,* 60.2 (1986) p 156.

28 A responsible treatment of these is M Perry (ed), *Deliverance* (London: SPCK, 2nd ed, 1996).